MONTHLY TO-DO LIST

JANUARY

FEBRUARY

MARCH

APRIL

MAY

JUNE

JULY

AUGUST

SEPTEMBER

OCTOBER

NOVEMBER

DECEMBER

NOTES

Weekly Planner

Monday

Tuesday

Wednesday

Thursday

Friday

Saturday

Sunday

to-do

Notes

NOTES

Weekly Planner

Monday

Tuesday

Wednesday

Thursday

Friday

Saturday

Sunday

to-do

Notes

NOTES

Weekly Planner

Monday

Tuesday

Wednesday

Thursday

Friday

Saturday

Sunday

to-do

Notes

NOTES

Weekly Planner

Monday

Tuesday

Wednesday

Thursday

Friday

Saturday

Sunday

to-do

Notes

NOTES

Weekly Planner

Monday

Tuesday

Wednesday

Thursday

Friday

Saturday

Sunday

to-do

Notes

Weekly Planner

Monday	*to-do*
Tuesday	
Wednesday	
Thursday	
Friday	*Notes*
Saturday	
Sunday	

NOTES

Weekly Planner

Monday

Tuesday

Wednesday

Thursday

Friday

Saturday

Sunday

to-do

Notes

NOTES

Weekly Planner

Monday

Tuesday

Wednesday

Thursday

Friday

Saturday

Sunday

to-do

Notes

Weekly Planner

Monday

Tuesday

Wednesday

Thursday

Friday

Saturday

Sunday

to-do

Notes

Weekly Planner

Monday

Tuesday

Wednesday

Thursday

Friday

Saturday

Sunday

to-do

Notes

NOTES

Weekly Planner

Monday

Tuesday

Wednesday

Thursday

Friday

Saturday

Sunday

to-do

Notes

Weekly Planner

Monday

Tuesday

Wednesday

Thursday

Friday

Saturday

Sunday

to-do

Notes

NOTES

Weekly Planner

Monday

Tuesday

Wednesday

Thursday

Friday

Saturday

Sunday

to-do

Notes

NOTES

Weekly Planner

Monday	**to-do**
Tuesday	
Wednesday	
Thursday	
Friday	**Notes**
Saturday	
Sunday	

Weekly Planner

Monday

Tuesday

Wednesday

Thursday

Friday

Saturday

Sunday

to-do

Notes

NOTES

Weekly Planner

Monday

Tuesday

Wednesday

Thursday

Friday

Saturday

Sunday

to-do

Notes

Weekly Planner

Monday

Tuesday

Wednesday

Thursday

Friday

Saturday

Sunday

to-do

Notes

NOTES

Weekly Planner

Monday

Tuesday

Wednesday

Thursday

Friday

Saturday

Sunday

to-do

Notes

NOTES

Weekly Planner

Monday

Tuesday

Wednesday

Thursday

Friday

Saturday

Sunday

to-do

Notes

NOTES

Weekly Planner

Monday

Tuesday

Wednesday

Thursday

Friday

Saturday

Sunday

to-do

Notes

NOTES

Weekly Planner

Monday

Tuesday

Wednesday

Thursday

Friday

Saturday

Sunday

to-do

Notes

NOTES

Weekly Planner

Monday

Tuesday

Wednesday

Thursday

Friday

Saturday

Sunday

to-do

Notes

NOTES

Weekly Planner

Monday

Tuesday

Wednesday

Thursday

Friday

Saturday

Sunday

to-do

Notes

NOTES

Weekly Planner

Monday

Tuesday

Wednesday

Thursday

Friday

Saturday

Sunday

to-do

Notes

NOTES

Weekly Planner

Monday

Tuesday

Wednesday

Thursday

Friday

Saturday

Sunday

to-do

Notes

Weekly Planner

Monday	**to-do**
Tuesday	
Wednesday	
Thursday	
Friday	**Notes**
Saturday	
Sunday	

Weekly Planner

Monday

Tuesday

Wednesday

Thursday

Friday

Saturday

Sunday

to-do

Notes

Weekly Planner

Monday

Tuesday

Wednesday

Thursday

Friday

Saturday

Sunday

to-do

Notes

Weekly Planner

Monday

Tuesday

Wednesday

Thursday

Friday

Saturday

Sunday

to-do

Notes

Weekly Planner

Monday

Tuesday

Wednesday

Thursday

Friday

Saturday

Sunday

to-do

Notes

Weekly Planner

Monday

Tuesday

Wednesday

Thursday

Friday

Saturday

Sunday

to-do

Notes

Weekly Planner

Monday

Tuesday

Wednesday

Thursday

Friday

Saturday

Sunday

to-do

Notes

Weekly Planner

Monday

Tuesday

Wednesday

Thursday

Friday

Saturday

Sunday

to-do

Notes

NOTES

Weekly Planner

Monday

Tuesday

Wednesday

Thursday

Friday

Saturday

Sunday

to-do

Notes

Weekly Planner

Monday

Tuesday

Wednesday

Thursday

Friday

Saturday

Sunday

to-do

Notes

Weekly Planner

Monday

Tuesday

Wednesday

Thursday

Friday

Saturday

Sunday

to-do

Notes

Weekly Planner

Monday	**to-do**
Tuesday	
Wednesday	
Thursday	
Friday	*Notes*
Saturday	
Sunday	

NOTES

Weekly Planner

Monday

Tuesday

Wednesday

Thursday

Friday

Saturday

Sunday

to-do

Notes

Weekly Planner

Monday

Tuesday

Wednesday

Thursday

Friday

Saturday

Sunday

to-do

Notes

Weekly Planner

Monday

Tuesday

Wednesday

Thursday

Friday

Saturday

Sunday

to-do

Notes

Weekly Planner

Monday

Tuesday

Wednesday

Thursday

Friday

Saturday

Sunday

to-do

Notes

NOTES

Weekly Planner

Monday	**to-do**
Tuesday	
Wednesday	
Thursday	
Friday	**Notes**
Saturday	
Sunday	

NOTES

Weekly Planner

Monday

Tuesday

Wednesday

Thursday

Friday

Saturday

Sunday

to-do

Notes

NOTES

Weekly Planner

Monday

Tuesday

Wednesday

Thursday

Friday

Saturday

Sunday

to-do

Notes

Weekly Planner

Monday

Tuesday

Wednesday

Thursday

Friday

Saturday

Sunday

to-do

Notes

Weekly Planner

Monday

Tuesday

Wednesday

Thursday

Friday

Saturday

Sunday

to-do

Notes

NOTES

Weekly Planner

Monday

Tuesday

Wednesday

Thursday

Friday

Saturday

Sunday

to-do

Notes

Weekly Planner

Monday

Tuesday

Wednesday

Thursday

Friday

Saturday

Sunday

to-do

Notes

Weekly Planner

Monday

Tuesday

Wednesday

Thursday

Friday

Saturday

Sunday

to-do

Notes

Weekly Planner

Monday

Tuesday

Wednesday

Thursday

Friday

Saturday

Sunday

to-do

Notes

NOTES

Weekly Planner

Monday

Tuesday

Wednesday

Thursday

Friday

Saturday

Sunday

to-do

Notes

NOTES

Weekly Planner

Monday

Tuesday

Wednesday

Thursday

Friday

Saturday

Sunday

to-do

Notes

NOTES

Weekly Planner

Monday

Tuesday

Wednesday

Thursday

Friday

Saturday

Sunday

to-do

Notes

Weekly Planner

Monday

Tuesday

Wednesday

Thursday

Friday

Saturday

Sunday

to-do

Notes

NOTES

Weekly Planner

Monday

Tuesday

Wednesday

Thursday

Friday

Saturday

Sunday

to-do

Notes

Weekly Planner

Monday

Tuesday

Wednesday

Thursday

Friday

Saturday

Sunday

to-do

Notes

NOTES

NOTES

NOTES

NOTES